D1213645

THANKSGIVING RECIPES

BY RONNIE ROONEY

PICTURE WINDOW BOOKS
a capstone imprint

Special thanks to Kathleen Curtin, for her time, her help, and her wonderful knowledge of all things related to Thanksgiving and the food that the Pilgrims and Natives may have eaten. –RR

Editor: Jill Kalz
Designer: Alison Thiele
Art Director: Nathan Gassman
Production Specialist: Sarah Bennett

The illustrations in this book were created with watercolor and pen and ink.

Picture Window Books
151 Good Counsel Drive
P.O. Box 669
Mankato, MN 56002-0669
877-845-8392
www.capstonepub.com

 All books published by Picture Window Books
are manufactured with paper containing at least
10 percent post-consumer waste.

Library of Congress Cataloging-in-Publication Data
Rooney, Ronnie.
  Thanksgiving recipes / written and illustrated by Ronnie Rooney.
    p. cm. — (Thanksgiving)
  Includes index.
  ISBN 978-1-4048-6283-8 (library binding)
  ISBN 978-1-4048-6722-2 (paperback)
  1. Thanksgiving cooking—Juvenile literature. 2. Cookbooks.
I. Title.
  TX739.2.T45R66 2011
  641.5'68—dc22
                        2010042332

Printed in the United States of America in North Mankato, Minnesota.
092010   005933CGS11

TABLE OF CONTENTS

THE THANKSGIVING STORY

The Pilgrims' first Thanksgiving in 1621 was different from the one we celebrate today. It lasted three days. Instead of football and parades, there were traditional dances and displays of marching and shooting skills. The Pilgrims and their guests, the Wampanoag, spent much of the time learning more about each other. But, of course, they also feasted!

Children played a big part in getting the meals ready. They plucked birds, fetched water, ground corn, and did other odd jobs. This Thanksgiving, help make your family's holiday the tastiest one ever. Pick a couple recipes from this book and get cooking! (And don't worry—you won't have to pluck any turkeys.)

TIPS

- Wash your hands before you start and whenever they get messy.

- Wash all fresh fruits and vegetables.

- To measure dry ingredients such as flour or sugar, spoon the ingredient into a measuring cup until it's full. Then use the back of a butter knife to level it off.

- To measure liquids, place a clear measuring cup on a flat surface. Slowly pour in the liquid until it reaches the correct line. Be sure to check at eye level.

GLOSSARY

coat—to cover with a thin layer

preheat—to turn on an oven before using; it usually takes about 15 minutes to preheat an oven

sprinkle—to scatter in small bits

stir—to completely mix ingredients with a spoon

toss—to mix ingredients together with your hands or two spoons

whisk—to quickly stir a mixture until it's smooth

METRIC CONVERSION CHART

1/2 teaspoon (2.5 milliliters)
1 teaspoon (5 milliliters)

1 tablespoon (15 milliliters)
2 tablespoons (30 milliliters)
3 tablespoons (45 milliliters)

1/4 cup (60 milliliters)
1/3 cup (80 milliliters)

1/2 cup (120 milliliters)
1 cup (240 milliliters)
2 cups (480 milliliters)

7 ounces (200 grams)
8 ounces (225 grams)
15 ounces (425 grams)

TEMPERATURE CONVERSION CHART

300° Fahrenheit (150° Celsius)
350° Fahrenheit (180° Celsius)
400° Fahrenheit (200° Celsius)

4

KITCHEN TOOLS

LARGE AND SMALL MIXING BOWLS

DINNER PLATE

SERVING PLATE

FORK

SMALL SPOON

LARGE SPOONS

BUTTER KNIFE

SMALL GLASS
BOWL

WOODEN SPOON

WHISK

TURNER

SERRATED KNIFE

APPLE CORER

KITCHEN SHEARS

MEASURING SPOONS

MEASURING CUPS

PAPER
BAKING CUPS

PAPER TOWELS

PLASTIC
SANDWICH BAG

PLASTIC WRAP

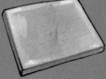
CUTTING BOARD

ROLLING PIN

OVEN MITTS

CROCK-POT

FRYING PAN

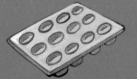
MUFFIN TIN

LARGE
MUFFIN TIN

SHALLOW
BAKING PAN

TURKEY CRACK-UPS AND CHEESE

Most likely, turkey and other wild birds were served at the Pilgrims' first Thanksgiving. But the birds weren't the stars of the show. Deer meat, or venison, was. The Wampanoag brought five deer to cook at the feast.

1 Spray cheese between the two round crackers, and put them together like a sandwich. This is the turkey body.

2 Put a dab of cheese in the center of the cracker body. "Glue" the oval cracker (turkey head) to it.

3 Have an adult cut the red pepper into quarters. Then cut one quarter into four long strips.

4 Have an adult slice the mozzarella stick into four even pieces.

5 Cut off the tip of the baby carrot.

6 Put a dab of cheese on the center of the plate. Place the cracker body and head on it.

7 Put some spots of cheese along the top edge of the cracker body—where the "feathers" will go. Next, add the feathers—red peppers first, then the broccoli, then the cheese.

8 Add the raisins for eyes, the carrot tip for a beak, and a red pepper strip for a snood.

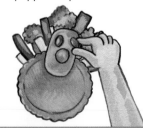

9 Add two spots of cheese at the bottom of the cracker body, and put the pretzels on for feet.

10 Pour ranch dressing below the turkey for dipping.

HAPPY GOBBLING!

Ingredients:

- 2 large round crackers
- 8-ounce can of spray cheese
- 1 oval cracker
- 1 red pepper
- 1 mozzarella stick
- 1 baby carrot
- 3 small broccoli florets
- 2 raisins
- 2 small pretzels
- ranch dressing for dipping

Tools:

- cutting board
- serrated knife
- kitchen shears
- dinner plate

ROASTY-TOASTY PUMPKIN SEEDS

Did you know the pumpkin is actually a fruit? It was one of the first foods to travel from America back to Europe.

1 Preheat the oven to 300 degrees Fahrenheit.

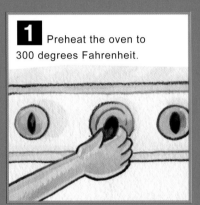

2 Have an adult cut off the top of the pumpkin using the cutting board and the serrated knife.

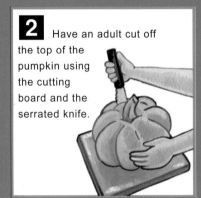

3 Use the large spoon to scoop out the seeds and pulp. Place in the large bowl.

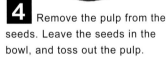

4 Remove the pulp from the seeds. Leave the seeds in the bowl, and toss out the pulp.

5 In the small bowl, mix together the salt, garlic powder, and Old Bay seasoning.

6 Coat the bottom of the shallow baking pan with the olive oil.

7 Sprinkle the seeds in one layer in the pan.

8 Sprinkle the seasoning mixture evenly over the seeds.

9 Have an adult bake the seeds for 15 to 20 minutes, until lightly browned.

Ingredients:

- 1 well-ripened pumpkin
- 1 teaspoon salt
- 1 teaspoon garlic powder
- 1 teaspoon Old Bay seasoning
- 1 tablespoon olive oil

Tools:

- cutting board
- serrated knife
- large spoon
- large mixing bowl
- small mixing bowl
- measuring spoons
- small spoon
- shallow baking pan
- oven mitts

LET COOL, AND ENJOY!

CORNY TURKEY DOGS

The Wampanoag showed the Pilgrims how to grow corn. Before that, the Pilgrims had never seen what we think of today as corn. The Wampanoag planted corn seeds in a mound and buried small fish alongside them. The fish made the soil better for growing crops.

1 Preheat the oven to 400 degrees Fahrenheit.

2 In the large mixing bowl, combine the corn muffin mix, egg, milk, and Bell's seasoning. Stir with the wooden spoon until the batter is a little lumpy.

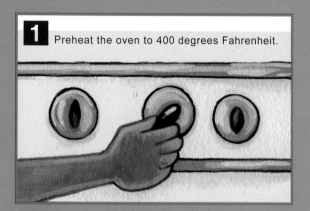

3 Line the muffin tin with paper baking cups.

4 Using the butter knife, cut each turkey dog into four pieces.

5 Carefully pour the batter into the baking cups.

6 Press a piece of turkey dog into the middle of each baking cup.

7 Have an adult bake the Corny Turkey Dogs 10 minutes or until golden brown.

DIP YOUR TURKEY DOGS IN MUSTARD. TASTY!

Ingredients:

- 8-ounce corn muffin mix
- 1 egg
- 1/3 cup milk
- 1/2 teaspoon Bell's seasoning
- 3 turkey dogs
- Dijon or yellow mustard for dipping

Tools:

- large mixing bowl
- measuring cups
- measuring spoons
- wooden spoon
- muffin tin
- paper baking cups
- butter knife
- cutting board
- oven mitts

11

TURKEY SALAD SANDWICH

The Pilgrims wouldn't have been able to make a turkey salad sandwich. Why? No bread! At the time of the Pilgrims' first Thanksgiving, in 1621, they hadn't grown any wheat to make bread yet!

Main Dishes

1 Use the butter knife to cut the turkey meat into small cubes.

2 Crush the cranberries with a fork.

3 Use the kitchen shears to cut the green onions into small pieces.

4 In the large mixing bowl, combine the mayonnaise, mustard, dressing, lemon juice, crushed cranberries, green onions, and salt.

5 Add the turkey and mix until coated.

6 Cover with plastic wrap, and refrigerate the salad for one to two hours.

7 Now prepare your sandwiches. On a slice of bread, place a piece of lettuce, a scoop of turkey salad, and pepper to taste. Top with another slice of bread. Repeat for the second sandwich.

ADD PICKLES AND CHIPS FOR A REAL TREAT!

Ingredients:

- 2 cups leftover turkey meat
- 1/4 cup cranberries
- 1/4 cup green onions
- 1/2 cup mayonnaise
- 2 tablespoons Dijon mustard
- 1/4 cup Italian-style dressing
- 1 teaspoon lemon juice
- 1/2 teaspoon salt
- 4 slices wheat bread
- 2 large pieces lettuce
- black pepper (optional)

Tools:

- cutting board
- butter knife
- measuring cups
- fork
- kitchen shears
- large mixing bowl
- measuring spoons
- wooden spoon
- plastic wrap

HARVESTTIME SALAD

The Pilgrims didn't have salad in a bag. In fact, they probably didn't even have lettuce! Cabbage was about the closest thing they had. Most likely, though, the Pilgrims wouldn't have eaten cabbage raw, like a salad. They liked their vegetables cooked.

1 Place the mixed greens in the large bowl.

2 Pour the dressing over the greens, and toss to coat.

3 Have an adult cut the apple and pear into bite-size chunks.

4 Move the greens to a serving plate.

5 Sprinkle the raisins, dried cranberries, pumpkin seeds, and sunflower seeds on top.

6 Top with the apple and pear chunks.

7 Sprinkle cheese over the salad.

PERFECT WITH A SLICE OF FRESH, WARM BREAD.

Ingredients:

- 7-ounce bag mixed salad greens
- 1/2 cup raspberry vinaigrette dressing
- 1 apple
- 1 Bartlett pear
- 1/4 cup raisins

- 1/4 cup dried cranberries
- 1/4 cup pumpkin seeds
- 1/4 cup sunflower seeds
- 1/2 cup shredded cheddar cheese

Tools:

- large mixing bowl
- measuring cups
- two large spoons
- cutting board
- serrated knife
- serving plate

GRILLED CHEESE AND GOBBLER

The Pilgrims had little cheese or milk. They might have made goat's milk cheese from the few goats they brought from England. We're a bit luckier. We can go to the deli and pick out cheeses from just about anywhere in the world!

1 With the butter knife, thinly spread butter on one side of each slice of bread.

2 Spread mustard on the other sides.

3 Place one bread slice butter-side down. Layer the turkey and cheese on top.

4 Have an adult cut two or three thin slices of tomato.

5 Place the tomato slices and the basil on top of the meat and cheese.

6 Top with the other slice of bread, butter-side up.

7 Put two pats of butter in the frying pan, and have an adult turn the heat to medium.

8 Once the pan is hot, use the turner to gently place your sandwich in the pan. Cook for three to four minutes.

9 Have an adult help you flip the sandwich with the turner. Cook for another three minutes.

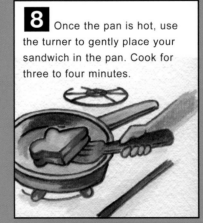

DELICIOUS WITH PICKLES AND CHIPS.

Ingredients:

- 2 slices wheat bread
- butter
- 2 tablespoons Dijon mustard
- 2–3 slices deli turkey
- 2–3 slices cheese (American or your favorite)
- 1 tomato
- 2–3 pieces fresh basil

Tools:

- cutting board
- butter knife
- measuring spoons
- serrated knife
- frying pan
- turner

17

ACORN DoNUT HOLES

The Wampanoag enjoyed eating acorns and other nuts. They roasted them and then ground them up with a mortar and pestle. The ground-up nuts were used for such things as thickening soup. It's a good bet these acorns are a bit tastier!

1 Using the butter knife, frost the top third of each of the donut holes.

2 Put the candy bar in the plastic sandwich bag, and place the bag on the cutting board. Use the rolling pin to gently crush the candy into small pieces.

3 Empty the bag onto the cutting board. Carefully roll the frosted part of each donut hole in the candy pieces.

4 With the kitchen shears, cut the licorice stick into 1/4-inch (6-millimeter) pieces.

5 Stick the licorice "stem" into the center of the frosted area of each donut hole.

Ingredients:

- 6 donut holes
- 1 can chocolate frosting
- 1 chocolate wafer candy bar (for example, Kit Kat®)
- 1 chocolate licorice stick

Tools:

- butter knife
- plastic sandwich bag
- cutting board
- rolling pin
- kitchen shears

GRAB A BIG GLASS OF MILK, AND ENJOY!

CROCK-POT APPLES

"As American as apple pie." Well, not quite! The *English* actually introduced apples to America. And the first apple orchards didn't start popping up until around 1630. That was about 10 years after the Pilgrims' first Thanksgiving. So no hot apple pie at that meal!

Desserts

1 Preheat the Crock-Pot on high heat.

2 In the large bowl, mix together the brown sugar, oatmeal, pumpkin pie spice, cinnamon, vanilla, and butter. The mixture will be sticky and lumpy.

3 Have an adult hollow out the middle of each apple with an apple corer.

4 Fill each apple with the oatmeal mixture, packing it tightly.

5 Place the apples in the Crock-Pot.

6 Pour the orange juice into the bottom of the Crock-Pot.

7 Cover and cook for about two and a half hours, until the apples are soft and start to fall apart.

Ingredients:

- 1/4 cup brown sugar (firmly packed)
- 1/4 cup oatmeal
- 1 teaspoon pumpkin pie spice
- 1 teaspoon cinnamon
- 1/2 teaspoon vanilla
- 3 tablespoons butter
- 4 apples (Gala or McIntosh work best)
- 1/3 cup orange juice
- vanilla ice cream for topping

Tools:

- Crock-Pot
- large mixing bowl
- measuring cups
- measuring spoons
- wooden spoon
- cutting board
- apple corer

21

MINI FRUIT COBBLERS

Unlike us, the Pilgrims didn't have to wait until they finished dinner to eat dessert. They would eat something sweet with their meat and vegetables. But their desserts weren't really all that sweet. The Pilgrims used small amounts of sugar. Sugar cost a lot of money and had to be shipped from England.

1 Preheat the oven to 350 degrees Fahrenheit.

2 In the large mixing bowl, whisk together the milk, flour, sugar, vanilla, and cinnamon.

3 Place the butter in the glass bowl and cover with a paper towel. Have an adult heat the butter for about one minute in the microwave, until the butter is melted.

4 Have an adult slowly pour the melted butter into the flour mixture. Whisk constantly.

5 Spray the muffin cups with vegetable spray.

6 Pour batter into each cup, filling each about half full.

7 Top each with 1/3 cup blueberries.

8 Have an adult bake the fruit cobblers for 25 to 30 minutes, or until golden brown.

Ingredients:

- 1 cup milk
- 1 cup self-rising flour
- 1 cup sugar
- 1 teaspoon vanilla
- 1/2 teaspoon cinnamon
- 1 stick butter
- vegetable spray
- 15-ounce package frozen blueberries
- whipped cream for topping

Tools:

- large mixing bowl
- measuring cups
- measuring spoons
- whisk
- small glass bowl
- paper towels
- oven mitts
- large muffin tin

TASTES TERRIFIC WITH WHIPPED CREAM!

READ MORE

Lassieur, Allison. *The Voyage of the Mayflower.* Graphic Library:
Graphic History. Mankato, Minn.: Capstone Press, 2006.

Philbrick, Nathaniel. *The Mayflower and the Pilgrims' New World.*
New York: G.P. Putnam's Sons, 2008.

Plimoth Plantation, with Peter Arenstam, John Kemp, and Catherine
O'Neill Grace. *Mayflower 1620: A New Look at a Pilgrim Voyage.*
Washington, D.C.: National Geographic, 2003.

INTERNET SITES

FactHound offers a safe, fun way to find Internet
sites related to this book. All of the sites on
FactHound have been researched by our staff.

Here's all you do:

Visit *www.facthound.com*

Type in this code: 9781404862838

LOOK FOR ALL THE
BOOKS IN THE
THANKSGIVING SERIES:

Life on the Mayflower
The Pilgrims' First Thanksgiving
Thanksgiving Crafts
Thanksgiving Recipes
Thanksgiving Then and Now

Super-cool
stuff!

Check out projects, games and lots more at
www.capstonekids.com

INDEX

24